Apostle Paul Speaks from Heaven:
A Divine Revelation

Matthew Robert Payne

This book is copyrighted by Matthew Robert Payne. Copyright © 2018. All rights reserved.

Any part of this book can be photocopied, stored, or shared with anyone for the purposes of encouraging people. You are free to quote this book, use whole chapters of this book on blog posts, or use this book for any reason if it is to spread the message of Jesus with this world. No consent from the author is required of you.

Please visit http://personal-prophecy-today.com to sow into Matthew's writing ministry, to request a personal prophecy or life coaching, or to contact him.

Cover designed by akira007 at fiverr.com

Edited by Lisa Thompson at www.writebylisa.com You can email Lisa at writebylisa@gmail.com for your editing needs.

All scripture is taken from the New King James Version unless otherwise noted. Copyright © 1982 by Thomas Nelson, Inc. Used by permission. All rights reserved.

The opinions expressed by the author are not necessarily those of Christian Book Publishing USA.

Published by Christian Book Publishing USA.

Christian Book Publishing USA is committed to excellence in the publishing industry. Book design Copyright © 2018 by Christian Book Publishing USA. All rights reserved.

Paperback:

Hardcover:

Dedication

To Nicola:

First of all, I want to dedicate this to Nicola as she is a very dear friend of mine. She has taken the time to speak with me and encourage me for many hours. She knows my weaknesses and faults and still loves me with an unconditional and unwavering love. I love you, Nicola.

Acknowledgments

Jesus:

I want to thank you for being my lifelong friend and for never deserting me, no matter how dark my life became. You led me into some great adventures, like writing this book.

Holy Spirit:

I want to thank you for leading and teaching me. You are a great teacher, better than I could ever be. I want to thank you for setting up this interview with Paul and helping with it.

Father:

Thank you for loving me and entrusting me with this life that I am living. Thank you for revealing my purpose to me and leading me toward accomplishing it. Thank you so much for your Son, Jesus. Thank you for everything that you have done in my life.

Lisa Thompson:

I want to give special thanks to Lisa for editing this book of mine. You take my simple words and transform them to make me seem smarter than I really am. If you have any editing needs, Lisa can be contacted at writebylisa@gmail.com

Nicola:

I want to thank Nicola for being part of my team as a proofreader. I want to thank you for all the work that you did with this book to polish and improve it. I want to also thank you for some of the questions in this book.

Mary:

I want to thank you for being my friend and for supplying some of the questions for this book.

Friends:

I want to thank Lisa, Nicola, Mary, Wendy, Laura, David Joseph, and Michael Van Vlymen for your friendship and how you have impacted my life.

Mom and Dad:

I want to thank my mother and father for all the love that they have given me. I am a product of your love.

Readers and ministry supporters:

I want to thank the readers of my books and my ministry supporters for the funds that you have given me to publish books. I want to thank the anonymous ministry supporter who gave me money for this project. I live to educate people, and I thank both my readers and the supporters of my ministry because you make life worth living.

Table of Contents

Dedication 3

Acknowledgments 4

Matthew's Question 10

Question 1 – How do you feel about being here today? 10

Mary's Questions.. 12

Question 2 – Hebrews 12:1 talks about a great cloud of witnesses in heaven. Kat Kerr describes a portal where saints can watch loved ones on earth. Can you talk about these witnesses and the balconies of heaven? 12

Question 3 – In 2 Corinthians 12:7, you talk about a "thorn in the flesh." Can you tell us what this thorn was and if you ever got upset at God because he wouldn't remove it? 14

Question 4 – How closely did the movie, *The Apostle Paul*, come to accurately describing your life and your relationship with Luke?........... 17

Question 5 – You talk a lot about God's grace toward us in the New Testament. How do you feel about the different messages about grace being taught today? 19

Question 6 – What advice do you have for believers in the twenty-first century?... 22

Question 8 – What do you love most about heaven, and what is your favorite thing to do there? 27

Question 9 – Can you describe your relationship with the apostles and how it felt not to be trusted at first after your conversion on the road to Damascus?.. 30

Question 10 – In 1 Timothy 1:15, you wrote, "Christ Jesus came in to the world to save sinners, of whom I am chief." Can you talk about why you felt this way? 33

Question 11 – We read in 2 Corinthians 5:8 that "to be absent from the body is to be present with the Lord." How hard was it for you to remain on earth when you longed to be in heaven with the Lord? 36

Question 12 – Can you explain what you meant in 1 Timothy 2:12 when you write about women being silent in church? 39

Nicola's Questions 42

Question 13 – What are some of the most important things you learned in your life that you would want Christians to know? 42

Question 14 – What was your biggest revelation regarding the differences between Christianity and the religious law you were taught under Gamaliel? 44

Question 15 – You spoke about sin and grace in Romans 6. "What shall we say then? Shall we continue in sin that grace may abound?" (verse 1). What would you say to those preaching or believing in the extreme grace doctrine or greasy grace? 46

Question 16 – You speak on divisions in the church in 1 Corinthians 3. What would you say to Christians today about divisions in the church and unity? 48

Question 17 – In 2 Corinthians 11, you speak of your sufferings for Christ. What enabled you to endure all these things, and what would you say to those in the persecuted church today? 51

Question 18 – Why is it important to please God and not men, and how do you learn to be this way? 54

Question 19 – In Ephesians 2:8–9, you talked about how we are saved by grace and not works but that God created us to do good works. What would you say to Christians about the difference between accepting God's gift of grace and doing works but not doing works to earn salvation? 56

Question 20 – What went through your heart and mind as you were imprisoned, and what kept you going? 58

Question 21 – What do you love most about the Lord Jesus, Father God, and the Holy Spirit? 60

Matthew's Questions 62

Question 22 – What do you think about people using your words to prove their point when their point is error? How do you feel about that? 62

Question 23 – Do you think that people should learn to speak to the Trinity and have a wonderful relationship with them in addition to reading the Bible? 64

Question 24 – What are some things that Jesus said to you that encouraged you when you were on earth? 67

Question 25 – You have shared that you lived a supernatural life on earth. Do you feel everyone should live this sort of life? 69

Question 26 – What do you say to people that find your teachings hard to understand? What should they do? 71

Question 27 – Have you seen the future of earth from heaven? What does it look like? 73

Question 28 – How does a person make a mark on society like you did? 75

Question 29 – What are your final words? 78

Learn how to have back-and-forth conversations with Jesus in the following books: *How to Hear God's Voice: Keys to Two-Way Conversational Prayer* by Matthew Robert Payne, *Hearing God's Voice Made Simple* by Praying Medic, and *God Speaks: Perspectives on Hearing God's Voice* by Praying Medic 78

I'd love to hear from you 80

How to Sponsor a Book Project 82

Other Books by Matthew Robert Payne.. 83

About Matthew Robert Payne.. 86

Matthew's Question

Question 1 – How do you feel about being here today?

I'm excited! It's exciting to come down, to work, and to speak to the readers. Once again, you're going to use your friends to ask me questions. You have questions from Mary and Nicola, and then you are going to ask some questions that you personally came up with.

I'm in a good mood right now. We don't really have bad moods in heaven. Heaven is quite different. The atmosphere of heaven changes your whole attitude and your whole outlook, but I'm very positive about what I have to say, and I'm trying to talk you into going through all eleven of Mary's questions today and not just stopping at six like you planned to do.

I have been watching your life, and I've been watching you as you participate in the first stages of healing in counseling. I'm very proud of you. I'm proud that you can continue to press on and do interviews with saints. You were told by the Holy Spirit that I would be the next saint to interview. You have prepared yourself, and you came to this interview in the right frame of mind.

I'm satisfied that you will be a good conduit of what I have to say. You haven't made up your mind about the answers to my questions. You are quite relaxed and able to listen to what I have to say. You are very open to the answers that I will share with you and the readers. I'm really confident that people will come to love this book and be convinced that I was actually speaking.

I am a very confident person. I speak with authority. When I'm in heaven, I speak with much authority. I don't want to use authority to override people's natural ability to think. I don't want to use my authority to push people down or to distract them from what they think is the truth. I just want to speak with honesty and clarity and say what's on my mind.

I have many things to say to you in the context of answers to these questions that I have been asked. I have many emotions running through me with the subject matter that will be covered. I enjoy living in heaven. I've visited you before, Matthew. In the book, *Great Cloud of Witnesses Speak*, I did an interview with you, and it was the longest interview in that book. I had quite a bit to say. That was very encouraging to you.

At that time, you could record sessions on YouTube that ran for hours. At the moment, you can't do that. It would be easier for you if we could just upload one file and have it all typed out. You have to split this into ten-minute segments because of how you're restricted.

You are aware that I've been here before. I've been to your house. Of course, you have new furniture. Your whole world is looking cleaner. I enjoy meeting you and being in your presence. I came to you and spent time with you in the last couple of days, sort of introducing myself to you and getting you used to my company. I hope that you're comfortable now. You've used this question as a warm up of spirit to spirit so that you understand me. We'll leave this question and go on to the questions that Mary has put together.

Mary's Questions

Question 2 — Hebrews 12:1 talks about a great cloud of witnesses in heaven. Kat Kerr describes a portal where saints can watch loved ones on earth. Can you talk about these witnesses and the balconies of heaven?

Every saint in heaven has loved ones on earth, and they all have varying degrees of access to the saints on earth. Sometimes the saint in heaven can even leave heaven and go to earth. You'll notice that people say in movies and TV shows and to you face-to-face that they feel their father or other family member around them, and they feel that person's presence. Sometimes the saint has actually left heaven and comes to that person as a presence in their life.

Kat Kerr speaks of balconies where people can publicly go and look down through a portal on earth and watch their loved ones. Every saint also has a TV in their own house and can turn to a certain channel and watch their son or their daughter or their loved one on what resembles a TV screen. Saints from thousands of years ago will also watch those with whom they are involved and whom they will impact.

In Matthew's other books, each saint has like an iPod in heaven where they are taught and their lessons are stored. Well, we have modern technology in heaven, which looks like what you have on earth.

Saints have a TV channel, a TV screen where they can watch their relatives on earth. They don't have to go to those balconies to see their loved ones.

Matthew has taken people to heaven and has been in the person's heavenly mansion and directed them to look at the TV screen in their mansion. They have been able to see Matthew and the person he is taking to in heaven on the TV screen. They can see themselves back on earth.

Saints can view their loved ones on earth in these two ways: through the balconies and the TVs. Right now, many saints in heaven are watching Matthew record this book. They are seated in their houses in heaven, tuned in, and excitedly watching Matthew sit at his computer desk and record this book. They can see me standing by his side dictating this, and they are happy that this record is going forth.

Saints in heaven have something similar to a TV guide. The TV guide is digital like an iPod. It brings up upcoming events in the lives of their loved ones. For example, their loved one will be baptized, or their loved one will speak to their pastor about preaching, or their loved one will share a testimony, or their loved one will do something important.

All these important events are put in the TV guide so that a saint can tune the TV in real time at the same time as the event happens on earth. They can be directed by the guide and turn on the TV and watch their loved one's special event.

Everyone interested in that event will be looking on. Of course, they will all go to the balcony in heaven and watch together, or they might sit in their individual houses and watch. Matthew and everyone has special events on earth, events that his relatives and that other saints in heaven would be interested in seeing.

They are told about the events through the computerized guides. Then they can tune in on the TVs in heaven and watch the event as it unfolds. Heaven has lots of YouTube and plenty of videos. They can also use playback on the events as well and replay what they saw again and again.

A saint on earth will do something significant, and their relative will usually watch. But if the saint happened to miss the event or if the saint in heaven wanted to replay the event because it was important, they can watch their television like YouTube and go back and watch it again.

Matthew has had some especially great moments in his life, such as his baptism. Saints in heaven like to replay that event and listen to it because it encourages them just like a father who pulls out a video and replays movies of his children. The father becomes nostalgic when watching the videos. The same thing is true about saints in heaven who re-watch events that have happened on earth.

You can be sure that if you have a loved one in heaven who has gone on before you, they are watching. Mary, your mother and father are watching you and listening to you even as you read this book. They are watching you as you're putting the questions together for this book. They are very interested in you, and they love you very much. You can be sure that heaven doesn't miss out on the important events in a person's life on earth.

Question 3 – In 2 Corinthians 12:7, you talk about a "thorn in the flesh." Can you tell us what this thorn was and if you ever got upset at God because he wouldn't remove it?

"And lest I should be exalted above measure by the abundance of the revelations, a thorn in the flesh was given to me, a messenger of Satan to buffet me, lest I be exalted above measure" (2 Corinthians 12:7).

For many, many years, ever since the Bible was printed, people have blamed this verse about Paul's thorn in the flesh for the various diseases that they've had. They have said to themselves that they simply have a thorn in the flesh like Paul had. But it's very dangerous to excuse disease in your life.

Jesus died, and his stripes, the marks in his body caused by the whips, were to remove pain and disease from your life. It's God's will for people to be healed. If people come up with an excuse why they can't be healed, such as claiming that they have a thorn in the flesh or that the sickness is to teach them a lesson, then that can become destructive to their Christian faith.

You'll notice that the verse uses the phrase, "a messenger from Satan," which sounds like a demon. It doesn't sound like disease. It's true that Satan causes disease, but I'm not sure that you could call a disease or a sickness a messenger. I wish that this book would be read by every Christian in the world so that we could answer this question.

The answer to the question is that a demon was released. The Lord allowed this demon to be released that used to travel from town to town and come upon people in each town where I preached. It caused the people to rise up against me and made trouble for me.

One way to explain this is that Matthew writes controversial books like this. From time to time, when he writes a controversial book, someone posts a bad review about the book. If you search under his name, Matthew Robert Payne, certain people have written a blog post against some of the books that Matthew has recorded.

They have been affected by this messenger from Satan, and they are raised up to ridicule Matthew and bring dishonor to his name.

The same was true for me. This messenger from Satan, this demon, used to manifest in people's lives wherever I went. Wherever I went, someone caused trouble and a disturbance. I was attacked and kicked out of the town. I was quite good at discerning spirits and had a gift for it. Every time this person was affected with this messenger, I knew that the same spirit was causing the trouble.

So I asked the Lord if he could do something about this spirit. I asked him if he could remove this thorn in my flesh. The reason it's called a thorn in the flesh is because it attacked my flesh, my carnal nature. It didn't please my flesh, my body, but it attacked my flesh life, my carnal life. It caused me a lot of pain and distress.

The thorn was spiritual, so it was effective. I could never get rid of it. It annoyed me, and the carnal, flesh part of me was upset that I was always hindered by this spirit.

That's an answer for people. It wasn't physically sticking into my flesh. It wasn't an actual thorn pressing into my flesh like the kind of thorn that pricks you when you pick up a rose. It affected my carnal flesh. I asked the Lord three times to remove it, and three times, he said no.

I was upset with God for a time. We all have our emotions, but I understood God's wisdom. I will also share with you that this messenger from Satan kept me humble and kept my feet on the ground because I'd been to heaven.

I went to heaven quite a bit. I spent a lot of time in heaven on heavenly encounters. These encounters are not all recorded in the scriptures, so this messenger traveled with me and kept me grounded and focused on the job at hand. The messenger also made sure that I moved around from town to town instead of staying in one town.

God had his purposes in my life. Modern-day preachers might experience the same sort of thing with people rising up in opposition in every town to them. If they're honest, they will agree that the same thing happens in their own ministry and in their own lives.

Question 4 – How closely did the movie, *The Apostle Paul*, come to accurately describing your life and your relationship with Luke?

The movie was well done and was a great depiction of what could have happened and of how I interacted with Luke. I was very open and loving. I was totally enraptured with the love and the grace of God. His love and mercy in my life totally transformed me from being legalistic without mercy into a loving, considerate, and compassionate person.

I had a lot of time for people, especially for those that wanted to serve God with me. I watched the movie with Matthew, and it was endearing to me and reminded me of Luke. Jim portrayed the character very well. I was pleased with it.

You could take the movie at face value and say that this was typical of my life. Of course, conditions in the Roman prison were much harsher than that. You only have to think that the Romans put a bucket in the corner of the prison to use as a toilet. You might realize that they could have more realistically shown the prison as dirtier with more poverty.

I was pleased that Luke wrote his Gospel and that he came and interviewed me and spent time with me to record the book of Acts and how I spread the gospel of Christ.

I want to remind people that the focus of Christianity isn't you. The focus of Christianity should always be your life in Christ and the way that Christ affects you.

Jesus reigned in my life. My life was totally dedicated and surrendered to him, and I accepted everything that he allowed to happen in my life. Part of that life was having people join me and spend time with me in prison. Solitary confinement can be extremely difficult, draining, and challenging. The highlight of my time in prison was when visitors came to see me.

Jesus said in the parable of the sheep and the goats, "I was in prison and you visited me. I was in hospital, I was sick and you visited me." (See Matthew 25:35–36.) When you're sick in a hospital, you want visitors. When you're suffering in prison, you want visitors.

I think the movie brought out that aspect really well. Jim, the actor who played the part of Luke, showed that I was very happy with Luke's visit and touched by his presence. I enjoyed spending time with him and recounting my life as I told of all the stages of my life and ministry with him.

He also helped me write some of the letters to the church that you find in the Bible. I wrote quite a few letters. I wrote many of these letters from prison as recorded in the Bible. I wrote other things that didn't make it into the Bible. But all in all, I was encouraging, loving, and transformed by the grace of God.

The Bible doesn't fully capture the kind of person that I was and the transformation that took place in my life. I'm so pleased and thankful to the Holy Spirit and his influence in my life. The Holy Spirit is to be honored and respected and given due glory for the role that he plays in each individual's life. He was a school master and trained me, changed me, and directed me to do everything that I did and was responsible for.

I want to personally thank the Holy Spirit. I want to also thank Jesus for being my Savior and for appearing to me on the road to

Damascus and changing the course of my life. Without that experience, I would have just been a wretched man. I'm so thankful to Jesus.

Since we're on this point, I want to say that I enjoyed the movie, *The Apostle Paul*, and the work that the producers, directors, and actors did. The movie was an accurate depiction of my interactions with Luke two thousand years ago. I will be well honored in heaven for the production of that movie.

Question 5 – You talk a lot about God's grace toward us in the New Testament. How do you feel about the different messages about grace being taught today?

First of all, I'd like to say that Jesus Christ is and should be the focus of your Christianity. Everything that Jesus said and did should be responded to and obeyed. A number of people in the grace camp today, part of what is called extreme grace or greasy grace, teach that Jesus was preaching an extreme form of legalism. They further teach that as believers, when we're saved by his blood, we no longer need to obey Jesus.

This didn't take Jesus by surprise because Jesus himself said that anyone who causes a little one to stumble should have a millstone tied around his neck. (See Matthew 18:6.) Jesus knew that people would teach a form of grace that said that obeying him was a type of unnecessary works. You don't need works for your salvation, but you are saved by grace alone.

Jesus understood beforehand that people would go to that extreme measure and teach that you do not need to obey what he taught. They teach that there's more to the Christian life than just the life of Jesus. But I say that if you're going to be a follower and a disciple of Jesus, you need to listen, understand, and obey what Jesus taught.

If you're not prepared to follow Jesus and obey him, how can you be called a follower? A number of people today follow certain modern-day teachers who teach extreme grace. They don't obey Jesus. They don't consider what Jesus taught important. This is disturbing.

Certain people teach preterism, which means that Jesus Christ has already returned to earth and the book of Revelation has already been fulfilled.

Some people in the grace camp teach that there's no hell and no eternal suffering. That is shameful and disrespecting of the scriptures and even of Jesus. He spoke of Lazarus and the rich man in one of his parables or stories. (See Luke 16:19–31.)

As with any topic, there are degrees of truth regarding what is being taught. Of course, there's error in rule keeping and legalistic teaching. People who are religious need to be saved and shown the truth of the grace of Jesus Christ and be free from rule keeping and from the false belief that God is an angry God. They need to be set free from these things.

They need to be careful that they don't swing too far the other way on the pendulum and land in a place of extreme grace where people are led toward error.

I'm upset. I understood that there would be heresy, false teaching, and false teachers in the earth in the last days. They say that the book of Revelation has already been fulfilled, that there's no hell, and that there's no need for repentance. They teach that you only have to repent to become a Christian and that you don't need to later repent of individual sins or live a holy life because that's a mission of works. These teachings are all errors.

The extreme grace camp teaches that performing any works is religion. They teach that any effort to show that you're saved by foundational spiritual works is futile. This is a scary teaching because my letters quite clearly say that we're created to do good works, that God's grace was provided so that we would fulfill the works that we are prepared for.

"For by grace you have been saved through faith, and that not of yourselves; it is the gift of God, not of works, lest anyone should boast. For we are His workmanship, created in Christ Jesus for good works, which God prepared beforehand that we should walk in them" (Ephesians 2:8–10).

You might not need to do works to be saved, but if you're truly saved, you'll do works, works that manifest the fruit of who you are. It's scary that many people, many well-recognized teachers in the body of Christ, are teaching extreme grace that says that good works are wrong and that holiness is a work of the flesh. Please see the book, *Hyper-Grace: Exposing the Dangers of the Modern Grace Message*, by Dr. Michael L. Brown.

If you're caught up in some of this teaching or following some of it, you might be alright spiritually. I don't want to make a blanket statement about everyone preaching grace because I was a big preacher of the grace of God. But you will find that my teaching was balanced and strongly rooted in holiness and in forsaking sin.

I spoke about the fruit of the Spirit and the lust of the flesh and how we have to forsake the lust of the flesh. My teaching was balanced, but people with an agenda to teach extreme grace will find some of my verses to back up what they say. People who want to teach legalism will find other verses to back up what they say.

It's important to stay true to how the Holy Spirit leads you.

Question 6 – What advice do you have for believers in the twenty-first century?

This is a wonderful question that I'd be pleased to answer, Mary.

If you've been reading this book and listening to what I have to say so far, you know that my focus is on Jesus Christ. I put Jesus first in everything that I say and do. God did not just send Jesus to die for your sins, but he modeled the life that everyone should try and emulate.

Jesus said in John 14:12 that he goes to his Father, but we will do greater works than he did.

"Most assuredly, I say to you, he who believes in Me, the works that I do he will do also; and greater works than these he will do, because I go to My Father."

Jesus was saying that he was not just our redeemer but a pattern to follow and emulate.

1 John 2:6 says, "He who says he abides in Him ought himself also to walk just as He walked."

John was saying that the way that you show you have a great relationship with Jesus is to walk like he walked. Matthew and his mother did some research at one point and found fifty commandments of Jesus.

These commandments were essentially what Jesus told us to do as his followers. We should not just say a prayer one day and become a Christian. We should actually follow Jesus. It's vital to understand what Jesus taught.

The fifty commandments can be found at this link, or if you're reading the paperback, you can search the fifty commandments of Jesus and look them up. Matthew Robert Payne wrote an Ezine article to describe these commands. You can print out the list of commandments and put it on your fridge. Read them and meditate on them and obey them.

I feel that one of the most important things that you can do as a believer is to emulate Christ and to be Christ in your situation. Of course, you can learn to prophesy, which is good as it encourages people. Every person who is a Christian can learn to prophesy. You can also learn to heal, which will help and encourage people.

What is most important is that you have the truth of Jesus Christ so that when people meet you, they meet a little Christ. Jesus taught many things when he shared his parables. A good understanding of Jesus's parables and a lifestyle of obedience to the lessons that he taught in his parables is essential for the Christian life.

You can read more about his parables and how to practically apply them in the book, *The Parables of Jesus Made Simple: Updated and Expanded Edition*, written by Matthew Robert Payne.

Matthew shares a lot of his life in his book, including his sins, his journey, and his struggles. He uses the context of his life to share some revelation along with the understanding of Jesus's parables. Once you learn the combination of Jesus's commands and parables, you will be set on a path toward an obedient lifestyle like Jesus.

In order to live the best possible Christian life, you need to be led by the Spirit. One way to be led by the Spirit and to be used by the Holy Spirit is to try and practice Jesus's commands. You'll find that you'll have to call on the Holy Spirit for his empowerment to obey the commands because the commands are almost the opposite of the way that you would normally act.

Jesus commands us to go the extra mile. This means if a person asks you to help them move from their house, you will offer to help them pack and unpack their boxes before and after you help them physically move their things.

If you had the discipline to go the extra mile in your life, you'd always call on the Holy Spirit for his empowerment to help you fulfill that commandment. If you start with the commands of Jesus, you'll find that you'll continually ask the Holy Spirit for his help and his empowerment. Over time, you'll learn to be led and directed by the Holy Spirit.

As you understand scripture and learn what Jesus taught, and as you start to live your life the way that Jesus suggested and commanded, you'll find that you'll continually ask the Holy Spirit for advice and help. Slowly, it will become your nature to move and do everything through the power of the Holy Spirit.

As you walk in the Holy Spirit, you'll become more and more like Jesus. Matthew feels that up to 95 percent of Christians have no understanding of the commands of Jesus. If you read this book and you went to the article and printed it out and put it on your fridge and started to practice the fifty commandments of Jesus, you'll actually be in the top 5 percent of Christians. You'll be unique and different, and you'll stand out.

What else could I tell believers in the twenty-first century other than to obey Jesus? I would advise them to understand Jesus. In the following books, *Jesus Speaking Today* and *Finding Intimacy with Jesus Made Simple*, Matthew describes the life of Jesus more intimately, and you understand Jesus better after you've read those books.

The more you understand the person of Jesus and the more that you understand who Jesus is, the easier it is for you to become like him and behave like him. So I wish you all the best.

Question 7 – In 2 Timothy 3:12, you talk about the persecution that all who will live godly in Christ Jesus will suffer. What encouragement can you give to believers today on how to endure since you experienced much persecution and many trials?

Different levels of persecution exist. Depending on who you are, the level of persecution will change. Some people will really suffer a lot. Other people, who seem to have the same background and upbringing, will suffer a whole lot less.

Satan has his agenda in a Christian's life to convince a Christian that their life is unfair. At the time that Matthew was writing this book, he has begun counseling, which is scheduled to last about six months with two one-hour sessions a week. That's a lot of talking, a lot of counseling.

He found himself asking, "Why me?" A lot of his counseling relates to past generations and attacks of Satan against him. He was often asking, "Why do I have to suffer so much?"

A person has to read the Bible and understand that we serve a loving, a just, and a fair God. Satan will try and convince you that your life is unfair and that you've been treated unfairly and that other people are being treated better than you are. If he can convince you of that, he can diminish your zeal. He can take away the fiery passion of your relationship with Jesus. He can put out the flame that is burning within you.

I have said along with Jesus that those who follow Jesus will be persecuted. There are different levels of suffering and persecution that come to various people. Of course, if you are a Christian in

China or North Korea, you face a whole new level of suffering compared to what people suffer in the West.

But people in the West suffer as well. They have trouble with their parents or in-laws. They face financial or emotional issues. People in different nations have problems. When they become Christians, they face heavy persecution. Several Bible passages address this: James 1:2–8 and 1 Peter 4:12–19. Verses like these encourage people and spur them on and bring them to a new level in their faith.

Some bloggers say that Matthew is a false prophet or that he's weird and practicing necromancy. He faces all sorts of attacks. Other people have written bad reviews about him, but that's really nothing compared to his relationship with Jesus.

He has a treasured relationship with Jesus. Jesus can turn up any time in his life. Matthew can walk and talk with saints and angels. He has this blessed life. Because he's living a godly life in Christ, he can endure the attacks that come against him.

You can be sure that it hurts every time someone writes a scathing review of one of his books. You need to know that you can not only be attacked, but you can survive, depending on your relationship with Jesus. All I had was the Holy Spirit and the relationship that I had with Jesus.

I mentioned before that I'd had many heavenly visitations. I was a little like Enoch who spent a lot of time in heaven. When I was in prison, I spent a lot of my time there on heavenly encounters in the third heaven. I lived in the glory, which was one of the ways I endured attacks.

People have the birthright to go to heaven and experience heaven. Ephesians 2:6 says that you are seated in heavenly places. You should operate from a position of strength, of divine encounters. It's also very helpful when you're being persecuted to understand the true nature of God and the true nature of Jesus.

When you understand that they're fair, they're just, they're loving, and you have scripture verses to back that up, Satan can't put his two cents in as easily or convince you that life is unfair. It's harder for him to slide a wedge in between you and Christ.

Some people in China are going through unbearable suffering. But if you ask them, they prefer the life they have as they would hate to be lukewarm like many people in the Western church.

We must understand the scriptures and prophecies. We need to develop a two-way conversational relationship with Jesus and the Father. You can speak to the Trinity; you can hear from them, and you can be encouraged by them, not only by scripture and by teachings that you've heard in books and videos, but by Jesus himself in the midst of your trial, in the midst of your suffering.

To help sustain me when I was suffering, Jesus used to visit me and appear in visions and give me heavenly encounters. I lived through the worst of my suffering through my supernatural experiences. It's not fair that people don't understand that they can have supernatural encounters. I encourage you to pursue them with all that you have.

Question 8 – What do you love most about heaven, and what is your favorite thing to do there?

Well, my favorite thing about heaven is what I also loved about earth. I love the people. The people of heaven are all different. They're all saved, redeemed, and holy. They're all eager to learn.

If you've ever been a teacher or a preacher, you'll understand that there are a couple of types of audiences. Some aren't engaged or interested in what you have to say. You might struggle to preach in that situation when they're not receiving, which can be like pulling teeth.

Another type of audience is really eager and hangs onto your every word. They're really fun to preach to. The people of heaven are like the second audience. They're all eager to learn.

You might wonder to yourself what you could possibly learn in heaven. Well, you might think to yourself that what you have learned on earth is your journey on earth. Do you know everything there is to know already? Why do you go to church? Why do you read more books? Why are you reading this book? Why do you watch YouTube videos or listen to podcasts? Isn't it because you are hungry to learn?

The same is true in heaven. You don't arrive in heaven and know it all. Heaven is a continual journey of learning one precept after another. I teach in heaven, and I'm taught in heaven. In heaven, people like Enoch and Elijah have much wisdom to share, and I learn from them.

On earth, you have a memory. The function of your memory depends on your age and other factors. On earth, you forget things, which is natural. You only have to watch a movie that you've seen before. If you watch it five years later, you'll find that most of the movie is new to you. You feel like you haven't watched it before.

Well, the point I'm trying to make about heaven is that you have a great memory, and you remember everything you learn in heaven. You can apply it to your life in heaven.

Heaven is a remarkable place. Can you imagine learning every day in heaven and being able to apply what you've learned? Can you imagine sitting under teachers in heaven who have been there for more than two thousand years? They understand the culture of heaven and understand concepts at a truly deep and outstanding level.

I'm speaking in simple language here as I talk to people on earth, yet I can speak in a really profound way as I talk about the glory of God. I can talk about different aspects of God and really astound you. But I'm speaking through a simple person: Matthew. I'm speaking down-to-earth truths.

My favorite thing to do there is teach. I'm a teacher. Of course, no one needs to be healed in heaven. I don't have to do signs and wonders, but signs are done in heaven. Different things are done to amaze and shock people. I love to expound on the Word of God.

I also love speaking to people one-on-one. I like to sit down with the person over a drink and expound knowledge to them and answer their questions. People can have individual questions that might not have anything to do with what I was just currently teaching. They can ask those questions, and I can answer them.

I love the banquets. I love the official functions that we have in heaven. I love to eat. I love to see the pageantry. I love to see the guest speakers.

As a teacher, I love to be taught. I love it when we have a function and an official speaker. I love to listen to them. I just love people. I'm such a people person. That's why it was hard for me to be in solitary confinement because I just love people. I laid my life down on earth to serve to people, to be a servant to others.

Heaven is glorious, and you want to go there. You're forever learning there. You can become everything that you were destined to be on earth. If you missed your calling on earth, if you missed doing what you were born to do on earth, you will fulfill your destiny in heaven. You will have a purpose and a function. You will have a job that you really love.

I encourage you to invite Jesus into your heart and accept him as your Lord and Savior. Follow him and obey him. I encourage you to lay down and sacrifice your life for Jesus right now and become very obedient and Christlike. The closer you become to Jesus on earth, the less you have to learn in heaven. That's just the way it is.

I really love teaching people. I love people so much and love meeting them face-to-face. Like I've said, my favorite thing to do in heaven is to teach.

Question 9 – Can you describe your relationship with the apostles and how it felt not to be trusted at first after your conversion on the road to Damascus?

People might not understand this fully, but I was like Hitler to the Jewish Christians. I was as determined as Hitler was to destroy them. I had a reputation all across what was known as Asia in those days. I had a reputation across the whole world that I was bloodthirsty and after Christians. Christians could easily think that I pretended to have a conversion experience so that I could come in and be like a double agent and find out information and evidence about them to bring them to trial.

It was important for Christians in those days to rely on the Holy Spirit and be led by him because if they were led by their natural flesh, they would never trust me because I was ruthless in my ambition to destroy Christians. I came against the very light of God and wanted to snuff it out.

The apostles took some time to warm to me and to learn to trust me. Many of the apostles walked with Jesus. I had to go away for some years to have my encounters with Jesus and learn what the apostles knew. It was an uphill battle to become respected by the apostles.

It wasn't as though I had a normal conversion. It wasn't as though I went through a process like the following:

- The apostles had saved me,
- I became their student,
- I grew in fame,
- I was appointed as an apostle myself, and
- I went on to serve them with their teaching.

First of all, I was a Pharisee, a member of a group that had condemned Christ and crucified him. Then, I was this murderous zealot who had gone after Christians with a vengeance.

People had a hard time believing that I had transformed. Of course, we had the testimony of Ananias. He had prayed for my sight to be restored, and he realized that Jesus had done a miracle for me. He understood that I'd been converted, but you only have to look at Christian circles to see examples of people like Benny Hinn. He is a man after God's own heart, and he's doing his best to serve God. But countless numbers of people post on Facebook and write blogs, calling Benny Hinn a false prophet.

Benny Hinn wasn't a Pharisee, and he wasn't killing Christians. He's served to the best of his abilities and the best of his understanding, yet Christians still call him a false prophet and a false teacher, someone to be wary of. Yet he's doing everything in his power to serve God.

Well, I was the arch enemy. The best way to explain it is to imagine if Hitler were converted and if he suddenly said that he wasn't against the Jews anymore. Imagine if he weren't going to try to build his own race anymore but that he wanted to follow

Christ. It would take years before people trusted him. He'd have to really show through his works and through experience that he could be trusted.

That's how it was for me. I can understand why the apostles were wary. Of course, they could communicate with the Holy Spirit and be told by Jesus that I could be trusted. But it was best for me to withdraw for years and go and learn the gospel and receive the teachings that I would bring to the Body of Christ.

I needed time alone in the desert to study the transformation message that I was going to bring to the people. It was best for me and for the early church to withdraw and learn these things. I think if I would have started preaching and teaching right from the gate after my conversion, they might have been even more wary of me, which is understandable.

I had a solid relationship with Jesus and the Holy Spirit. I was duly informed as to what was going on in the minds of the apostles. You remember that Jesus used to be able to read people's minds and discern what people were thinking. The Holy Spirit could show me what the apostles were thinking, their frame of reference, and their understanding when it came to me.

I was prepared, and I wasn't embarrassed, ashamed, or upset that they held me at arm's length for a while. I had to prove myself and to show that I was preaching the true gospel and that I could be trusted. It's sort of funny to see that at the end of the day, my teachings and my words are recorded more in the Bible than any of the other apostles. John and Peter had some recordings, but my teachings take up most of what modern Christians call the New Testament. In that way, I had the last say, which was good.

I had a difficult path. As with anything, perseverance and endurance win out in the end. Anyone who's had it rough and still made it seems to shine with a brighter light than people do who had an easy time. I hope that answered your question, Mary.

Question 10 – In 1 Timothy 1:15, you wrote, "Christ Jesus came in to the world to save sinners, of whom I am chief." Can you talk about why you felt this way?

I addressed a lot of that when I answered the last question. I didn't kill six million Jews like Hitler did, but I was certainly an archetype of Hitler. I was one of the first people to come against Christians with a vengeance.

Satan is tireless in his pursuit to damage Christians. He used me powerfully to rise up against Christians in my zeal to wipe them out. Then he tormented me throughout the rest of my life for what I'd done and what I did.

I was very aware of my conversion. Jesus used a supernatural event and appeared to me in a vision and knocked me off my high horse, physically and spiritually. He spoke to me from the heavens. I knew that was supernatural. Jesus went out of his way to save me. Not every person is saved so supernaturally. I knew that if Jesus hadn't apprehended my life, I would have continued to be a zealous enemy of the Christian church. I said that I was the chief of sinners because I was aware of the evil within me.

Every single murder that I was responsible for haunted me. Every person that was put to death because of my orders, every person who'd been persecuted and arrested under my orders, haunted me. Their faces haunted me. *The Apostle Paul* movie depicts this by those people who were in my dreams. But the enemy did a major job on me. I was harassed by the enemy time and time again for what I'd done.

First, the enemy had me hunt people down. Then, when I found out that what I was doing was wrong, and I was converted, I was harassed by the enemy for what I'd done. Isn't it just like the enemy? He tempts you to do something. You go ahead and succumb to the temptation. Then he harasses you for what you did.

Matthew did something fifteen years ago that Satan still brings up and harasses him about. It's quite reasonable that you can confess your sins and be forgiven, and yet you can still be harassed by the enemy for something you did. I was very aware of what I had done to the early Christian church and what an enemy I was to them.

I was brutally honest with myself that what I'd done was despicable and against God. That's part of why I said I was the chief of sinners.

Of course, evil people have lived after me. For instance, Hitler has lived his life and was a bigger sinner than I was. I wouldn't say that I'm the chief of sinners in history, but at that point in time, when I lived, I felt that I was the worst.

That's what makes grace, the redeeming grace of Jesus, so beautiful and so amazing that even an enemy of the Christian faith can be changed and transformed into a light bearer, and that's what I became. I became a standard bearer of light. I took the light of the gospel of Christ to a very dark and decrepit world where they served foreign gods, the gods of their ancestors. It was a terrible time, not like your modern world.

I took the light of Christ into all those regions and countries and helped them to see that this man who lived in Israel and who ministered there for a short time was really the God of gods, the Son of God, and the Creator that they should be in touch with. I encouraged them to let go of their family gods and their nation's gods. I told them that they should serve the one true God, Jesus

Christ. I took that message of liberty, freedom, and power to the world.

I could write great scriptures through my understanding of Jesus and his love. I wrote the love chapter in 1 Corinthians 13. I could explain what the love of God is like. Matthew doesn't know any other description of love that's more perfect, including all the hundreds of songs he's heard on love, the sermons, the teachings, and how people talk about love. Nothing better encapsulates love than the scripture in 1 Corinthians 13.

"Though I speak with the tongues of men and of angels, but have not love, I have become sounding brass or a clanging cymbal. And though I have the gift of prophecy, and understand all mysteries and all knowledge, and though I have all faith, so that I could remove mountains, but have not love, I am nothing. And though I bestow all my goods to feed the poor, and though I give my body to be burned, but have not love, it profits me nothing.

"Love suffers long and is kind; love does not envy; love does not parade itself, is not puffed up; does not behave rudely, does not seek its own, is not provoked, thinks no evil; does not rejoice in iniquity, but rejoices in the truth; bears all things, believes all things, hopes all things, endures all things.

"Love never fails. But whether there are prophecies, they will fail; whether there are tongues, they will cease; whether there is knowledge, it will vanish away. For we know in part and we prophesy in part. But when that which is perfect has come, then that which is in part will be done away.

"When I was a child, I spoke as a child, I understood as a child, I thought as a child; but when I became a man, I put away childish things. For now we see in a mirror, dimly, but then face to face. Now I know in part, but then I shall know just as I also am known.

"And now abide faith, hope, love, these three; but the greatest of these is love."

You can understand that God is a loving God. His love is amazing and transformational. God doesn't celebrate wickedness; his love endures forever. His love is perfect. He saved me, and he made me into someone worthwhile. He propelled me into becoming a witness for him in the world, which gave me a lot of joy.

It also helped people when I told them that I was worse than they were. People could accept that they're worthy of Jesus Christ. Part of the reason that I said that I was the chief of sinners was to encourage everyone else to embrace Christ too.

Question 11 – We read in 2 Corinthians 5:8 that "to be absent from the body is to be present with the Lord." How hard was it for you to remain on earth when you longed to be in heaven with the Lord?

That's a great question, Mary. I shared in a previous question that I visited heaven multiple times. I really had a life like Enoch. I became tremendously close to the Lord Jesus, the Holy Spirit, and the Father in heaven. They invited me up to meet them and spend time with them, see heaven, see the angels, and visit other saints. I sat at the feet of Jesus, listened to him, had supper with him, and conversed with him.

It was hard to live on earth with all its sufferings. You're very aware of the beatings with rods, the whippings, the shipwrecks, and all the hard things that happened to me. We can quote that scripture here of all the things that I went through.

"Are they ministers of Christ?—I speak as a fool—I am more: in labors more abundant, in stripes above measure, in prisons more frequently, in deaths often. From the Jews five times I received forty stripes minus one. Three times I was beaten with rods; once I was stoned; three times I was shipwrecked; a night and a day I have been in the deep; in journeys often, in perils of waters, in perils of robbers, in perils of my own countrymen, in perils of the Gentiles, in perils in the city, in perils in the wilderness, in perils in the sea, in perils among false brethren; in weariness and toil, in sleeplessness often, in hunger and thirst, in fastings often, in cold and nakedness—besides the other things, what comes upon me daily: my deep concern for all the churches. Who is weak, and I am not weak? Who is made to stumble, and I do not burn with indignation?" (2 Corinthians 11:23–29).

When you look at this list of what I endured, you might wonder what sort of person could live through this. What sort of person would want to continue to live? If you had endured all of the things on this list, and you had experienced heaven before, how hard would it be for you to choose to stay on earth?

I said once that I preferred to be in heaven over staying on earth, but for the sake of people, I stayed on earth. But it's really hard and very trying. In this way, I'm similar to Matthew, and Matthew's similar to me. Matthew's had a really trying and hard life. So much of him desires to be in heaven, desires to be done with this life, and yet he stays to record and write books like this, and to touch people's lives and direct them to Jesus and to teach them about how to be strong Christians.

He stays for the people. It was the same with me. I had such a love for the people on earth. I shared that I still have a love for them. I stayed because of that love for the people, and yet it was very hard.

When it's really hot outside, you might go to a shopping center where it's air-conditioned. You might decide to go to the shopping center every day because you don't have air-conditioning in your house, and you just want to hang out at the mall where it's cool.

Well, you can compare the world to your house and outside without air-conditioning and imagine that the shopping center is in heaven. If you live in a hot world like that, you'd find reasons to go to the shopping center as much as you can. That's what I did when I was on earth. I spent a lot of time in heaven in the heavenly places.

I wrote about it and shared about it so that other people could understand the truth about the people's birthright. I wrote in Ephesians 2:6 that we are seated in heavenly places. But I used to go to my shopping center—heaven—as I've described as often as I could. I lived in the hot world. I experienced the heat and the sufferings of the world, but I used to camp out at the shopping center whenever I could.

You've asked a very important question, Mary, because not a lot of people in the West live such a hard life that they prefer to be in heaven. But a number of people do live that kind of life. They have an extremely hard life and yearn to be in heaven. As they read this book, it's important to understand that they will be in heaven for eternity. I've been in heaven for two thousand years, and I really enjoy it. My time on earth seems like a vapor and a mist, irrelevant compared to the time I've been here.

I want to encourage those people who are having a hard time on earth and tell you that heaven is going to be beautiful for you. You want to learn how to open your spiritual lives and actually learn how to go to heaven and spend some time there while you live on earth. You can be encouraged by Jesus, the Father, the Holy Spirit, the saints of heaven, and the angels.

Just understand that it's only a short while between now and when you'll be in heaven. Everything will pass away. Everything will be squared away. Jesus will come and wipe the tears from your eyes, and everything will be glorious.

I hope that you were happy with the answer to this question. It was incredibly hard to live life on earth.

Question 12 – Can you explain what you meant in 1 Timothy 2:12 when you write about women being silent in church?

Many have understood this to mean that women are not allowed to be preachers or leaders in the church. Matthew was going to skip this question and simply say that he couldn't answer it because there's so much controversy about it. Some men commonly believe that these verses are literal and use them as weapons to say that women can't be preachers. No matter how I answer this or what I say here, people will call my response into question, say that it's not scriptural, and disregard it.

My answer to the people who think that women can't preach is to just look at how Joyce Meyer is influencing the world. Consider her anointing. You can sense the anointing on a person because when you're tired, and you listen to the person, the person's preaching can actually wake you up. When you're not really focused and someone starts preaching, and you become extremely focused and attentive, that means that the person is anointed. Some people will read Matthew's books and say that they're anointed because they are page-turners and are really fascinating to read.

Where does the anointing come from? The anointing comes from the Holy Spirit. If Joyce Meyer can preach under the anointing, she's anointed by the Holy Spirit. Now my question to you skeptics is would the Holy Spirit empower someone if they were breaking the commands of the Bible? If they were acting contrary to the Bible, would the Holy Spirit empower that person?

The answer to that is no. People will always use what I wrote in those early days against women. At the time, they weren't regarded as equal to men. People will always try to use what I wrote to keep women down.

Another example of a woman in ministry who is very well respected is Heidi Baker. She operates in miracles and healing, such as healing hearing loss and blindness, and does all sorts of signs and wonders.

She's multiplied chicken and food. Once, she even multiplied presents—beads—for all the African girls. Heidi Baker said, "The girls want beads. Pray for beads." The woman serving said that they had run out of beads. Heidi said, "Pray over the bag."

The woman prayed over the bag and put her hand into it, and beads started coming out. Before that, no beads were in the bag. They'd run out. But Jesus supernaturally filled the bag with beads.

Heidi's done other miracles like that. She's a woman. Wherever she travels and speaks, she captivates audiences. Audiences are blessed and encouraged and come away with a touch from the Lord.

Something's wrong with those who teach against women in ministry. You have to look at those scriptures that I wrote and consider what's happening today with people like Patricia King and other women preachers. You should think to yourself that some aspect of those passages was misunderstood regarding the culture of that time and the culture of today.

I did say in Galatians 3:28 that there are no women or men, no slave or free under God. You can see that I wrote that verse also. When I say that there's no male or female but that we're all under God or one under God, you can understand that flies in the face of the other verses, and only one of them can be right.

The beauty of the Bible is that all throughout the Bible, verses seem to contradict each other. This creates a tension in the Bible that holds everything in balance. You can look at my writings and use portions to substantiate your very legalistic teaching. You can use certain portions of my writings to support a teaching on extreme grace. Or you can use verses in the Bible that I wrote to gain a real balanced understanding of holiness and righteousness. Everything depends on who's interpreting the Bible and what you're using to interpret it.

Just ask yourself if Joyce Meyer would be popular and have the success that she has and have the anointing on her life to change lives if she were wrong. Where would the anointing come from if she were a false teacher? I know some people think she's a false teacher, but some of those people are very mixed up. I hope that answers your question, Mary.

Nicola's Questions

Question 13 – What are some of the most important things you learned in your life that you would want Christians to know?

The number one thing that I learned in my life was how to love God and how to love people. I learned how to become Christ. I learned how to be influenced by the Holy Spirit to such a point that I became love incarnate. You will notice that I wrote the love chapter in 1 Corinthians 13 as I already mentioned. You would have to first experience that kind of love to be able to form a picture of what love is, to be able to write the love chapter. Not many Christians could confidently say that they had achieved that level of love in all their interactions with people.

I did achieve it. Not a lot is written about my personal life in the Bible and how I felt, but I did become love. John was the apostle of love and held up as such. But I was also an expression of God's love, a visible expression of the love of Christ.

Love conquers all. Love cancels out sin in people's lives. When people come against you and cause you trouble, few of them are loved by the person being attacked. The right kind of love cancels out every offense. People can't fight successfully against pure love. Pure love will always win out, no matter when it happens. Let me repeat that. Pure love will always win out.

I have many examples and many situations in my life that called for me to push myself and move into a position of love. When people caused commotion and had me stoned, I struggled to forgive the people who were throwing the rocks at me.

I survived the stoning, but it would have been difficult for many people to come to grips with their emotions and feelings for those who tried to kill you. I was indebted to the relationship that I had with the Holy Spirit. He was so proud of me, so very proud of me, that doing miracles came easily for me. Once again, through my love and through the compassion I had for people, God allowed me to heal people and do signs and wonders in their lives. When you have compassion for people who are sick and who need a miracle, it's like a conduit for the Holy Spirit to flow. The Holy Spirit flows down through your compassion and through your faith to heal a person.

Another lesson I learned was to endure and to persevere. I understood that my life had to go on despite the hardships that came against me. I had to learn to have an overcoming spirit and perseverance in my character.

I had many situations in my life that would have made an ordinary person give up, and yet I was so close to the Holy Spirit. We were really good friends. I feel that one of the keys to an abundant and successful Christian life would be for you to develop an intimate relationship with the Holy Spirit.

Through a close relationship with the Holy Spirit, you can learn to love, endure, and overcome. You have many opportunities as a Christian to display Christ and to be an example of him. Christ wants you to display him. He wants you to be a relevant, outstanding citizen wherever you go: in your workplace, in your place of worship, in your shopping centers, on the bus, or on the train. Jesus truly wants you to be like him and display him.

One key is that you can learn to love, and another key is that you draw close to the Holy Spirit and have a distinct and powerful relationship with him.

Question 14 – What was your biggest revelation regarding the differences between Christianity and the religious law you were taught under Gamaliel?

Once again, I have to bring this back to love; there is no law against the law of love, no law that contradicts the fruit of the Spirit. The fruit of the Spirit dominates, and there's no law against it, according to Galatians 5:22–23.

When living as a Pharisee in those days, others placed so much pressure on appearance. You might think that as a churchgoer today, you have to wear a veil or a mask and pretend that everything is okay. You are almost living a life of lying to your fellow Christians about who you are, that you're doing well, and that you have no problems.

Many people go to church, wear these masks, and pretend that everything is okay. As a Pharisee, I had to keep up appearances. There was no pretense or putting on an act. You either were obeying the law, or you weren't obeying the law. As a leader, you were held to the highest standard.

King David spoke in the psalms about loving the Lord and loving the precepts of the Lord and living his life in obedience to the law. He found a certain joy in obeying the law and being in right standing with God all the time.

Of course, we lived pre-Christ with no Holy Spirit, so your own will allowed you to obey the law, and there were many laws. Many Christians have no comprehension of how strict and how rigid it was. I came out of that. I needed the transition, the time in the desert, to come out of that strict practice, out of that legalism. But I went into a new way of behaving myself, which was to be led by the Holy Spirit and to act based upon the law of love. I had to ask myself: How did my actions show God that I loved him, and how did my actions show my neighbor that I loved him?

When I reached the stage where all my actions were defined by love, it was freeing. There was a freedom to it. There's no mistaking that love conquers all. There's no bondage or rigidity with love. Love has this freedom to soar like a bird.

I enjoyed moving and displaying my love to people. I preached a new message, a message that said you don't have to be bound up with the rigid law anymore. Instead treat God with honor and respect and revere him as the holy God and love your neighbor as you would love yourself.

The new way of loving was full of freedom and gave me space to go the extra mile with people. The law said what it said, and it had its expressions, but the ability to live by the law of love carried so much freedom and hope. Essentially that's what the gospel is. It's behaving and obeying the law of love.

I've said in the scriptures that the law has passed away, but I'd like to say that the rigidity of the law was an offense and difficult to live under. When you live under the law of love, when you engage with love as your central theme, you fulfill the law just like Jesus fulfilled the law. He fulfilled the law by living in love. He lived out his life by loving God and loving others.

We want to emulate Christ. To answer your question, my biggest revelation regarding the difference between Christianity and religious law is that Christianity is supposed to be a lifestyle of love.

Now there are different factions and divisions in Christianity. People fight and argue on Facebook about these different factions of Christianity.

Christians engage in so much rivalry, bad language, and bad behavior. They should be known by their love, and each individual must pursue love and the Holy Spirit to such an extent that they can live a perfect life.

Question 15 – You spoke about sin and grace in Romans 6. "What shall we say then? Shall we continue in sin that grace may abound?" (verse 1). What would you say to those preaching or believing in the extreme grace doctrine or greasy grace?

I want to say to you that many deceived people and those who believe lies are good people. They don't choose to willingly walk down the wrong path or decide to be evil through a specific choice. Many people on earth are trying to live the best life that they can.

Quite a few people have been taught the ways of extreme grace and the greasy grace doctrines. Teachers that they trust have taught them this, and they believe what they're teaching. They teach it with passion and love, and the proponents who believe it follow along like sheep, and they allow their shepherds to lead them into pasture that might not be healthy.

Matthew has dealt with those who believe in the extreme grace doctrine. But he has never personally heard of preachers saying that you can do whatever you like with no consequences.

Of course, I'm in heaven, and I've heard what people say and do. It's more what they don't say that causes trouble. For example, they say that repent means to turn around or change your thinking, and they preach that there's no need for repentance any more since you've been saved. That's wrong. When they teach that you're forgiven for your past, present, and all your future sins on the cross, that is right. All your future sins were forgiven on the cross, but you need to confess your sins and come clean with God when you do trespass.

Jesus said in the prayer that he prayed with his disciples in Matthew 6:12, "Forgive us our debts, as we forgive our debtors." Jesus modeled this prayer for us, asking God to forgive us of our sins. When you promote the teaching that you don't have to repent, this can allow someone to continue in a lifestyle of sin and never truly repent for sin. They actually need to be set free from those sins through the power of the Holy Spirit.

Things can get greasy, to use that word. A bit of grease might be mixed with the purity of the oil. This concerns me. Some grace preachers will say that you don't need to obey Jesus and what he taught. You have to do what Jesus taught because Jesus was showing people how to walk in love and how to live according to the law of love. He wasn't setting down his own law or bringing forth his own rigid set of rules. He was expressing the law in a more loving way, a more understandable and a more compatible way for people to live

When grace preachers say that you don't need to obey Jesus or that you don't have to do anything, that you don't have to perform works to inherit salvation, they do their followers great harm.

A lot of slippery teaching, a lot of greasy teaching exists in the church.

Of course, people can be based in the law and attached to the Old Testament and the modern expectations of going to church each week, tithing, praying each day, and regular Bible reading.

Religious activities can overtake people and bring them into places of shame and condemnation when they don't do these things.

Religious thinking can contain just as much error as extreme grace teaching. A balance is in the middle where you live a righteous and holy life. On one side, you respect the Lord, and you respect what was taught on the other side. You live with the freedom of being able to live according to the law of God.

I'm not sure if people fully understand this with all the teaching that they've heard. I'm not sure if they fully understand that we are called to love, called to a higher form of love. Christians are called to display love and exercise love in every interaction that they have, in everything that they do.

I think if Christians could lay hold of the law of love and walk in it, they would be a whole lot better off. It would correct some of the excesses that are seen in the extreme grace movement.

Question 16 – You speak on divisions in the church in 1 Corinthians 3. What would you say to Christians today about divisions in the church and unity?

Of course, when Jesus prayed in John 17 that Christians would be one as he and his Father are one, he wanted the church to be in unity. So many divisions exist in the church, which is unfortunate.

The modern church is run by individuals and certain people who like things their own way. They like to believe what they choose to believe. If people teach differently from their beliefs, they form factions and divisions based on teachings, on beliefs.

It's unfortunate that there is division. A whole lot more unity exists in the Christian faith than what most people understand. When we look from heaven, we don't see thirty thousand denominations. We see the Bride of Christ. When we look from heaven, we don't see different facets and streams of the Christian faith. We see one stream flowing together.

The more intellectual man has become, the greater access he has to reading material and the easier it is to disseminate information. This spreading of information causes more prevalent factions and divisions in the church.

Matthew believes that you can have a relationship with Jesus to such an extent that Jesus will introduce you to saints in heaven who can speak to you. Very few people in the church actually believe that. If Matthew was setting up a church that taught everything he walks in, only a few select Christians would join that church because so many people would have reservations about it. They would have reservations about meeting angels and speaking to angels. They would have reservations about Matthew giving people messages from the angels. They'd have reservations about producing books without hundreds of key texts referenced in the books. They'd have problems with different points that he preached or that he believed.

And so it goes on down the line; every leader has different understandings and different beliefs. Those beliefs and the individuality of each of those beliefs set people apart and cause division.

Division isn't necessarily bad. If I were to tell you that we were going to unify the church and that everyone in the church had to participate in masses like the Catholic Church, you probably wouldn't be happy. If we all had to sit through the liturgy, the readings, and the standing up and sitting down and kneeling, many Christians would cringe and refuse to participate. They would say, "I don't want to be part of that. I want the freedom to be able to worship in a service like I'm used to. I don't want to conform to that."

If Catholics were told that they couldn't have a Catholic mass anymore but that they had to worship God like a Pentecostal church with free worship and dancing and holding hands in the air and thirty-minute sermons and no liturgy and just a free-flowing service, they would cringe also.

What do you do with the Body of Christ? Could you honestly bring them together in unity? The only exception would be if the church came under persecution. If the church came under persecution, that would tend to unify Christians. If Christians had a common enemy who persecuted them, then you might find that Christians from every stream might stop to come together and be unified as a body.

If you look at disunity and division as a bad thing, it will upset you, but when you look at the fact that each person is an individual and individuals like to find what makes them happy, you'll find that division isn't necessarily always bad.

We know in heaven who is saved and who is coming to heaven. We understand the people who are on fire and those who are committed. We know those people across every denomination and every part of the church. People in every congregation and in every denomination are on fire for God.

We respect that. We wouldn't take a certain denomination because it's more on fire, and we wouldn't reject people in a dead denomination that's not on fire. Jesus weighs the hearts of everybody. He really does look at the heart of a person.

Before this question, Matthew thought division was a problem, but you'll understand now that a lot more can be taught through diversity. You wouldn't want every painter to paint in the same style. You wouldn't want every musician to sing the same style. So it is in the church. Jesus really loves the diversity that's found in the many parts of his Body.

Question 17 – In 2 Corinthians 11, you speak of your sufferings for Christ. What enabled you to endure all these things, and what would you say to those in the persecuted church today?

I endured my sufferings because of the relationship I had with God. I knew that God had a purpose for my life. I knew I was a powerful witness for God and until I was put in prison at the end of my life, I knew I had to persevere.

Perseverance in the midst of struggle is commendable. Peter said in 1 Peter 4:12–13, "Beloved, do not think it strange concerning the fiery trial which is to try you, as though some strange thing happened to you; but rejoice to the extent that you partake of Christ's sufferings, that when His glory is revealed, you may also be glad with exceeding joy."

A measure of glory can be released in the midst of trial. You can shine with the Isaiah 60 glow when you're being persecuted. I would tell people who are being persecuted to look full in the face of Jesus.

A classic hymn says it so well. "Turn your eyes upon Jesus. Look full in his wonderful face and the things of earth will grow strangely dim in the light of his glory and grace."[1]

I would implore people to develop the ability to see in the Spirit. You can learn how to do this by buying the books by Michael Van

---

[1] "Turn Your Eyes Upon Jesus," CCLI Song Search, https://us.search.ccli.com/songs/4338237/turn-your-eyes-upon-jesus. Accessed June 11, 2018.

Vlymen and Praying Medic. Both books will help you develop your ability to see in the Spirit so that you can see Jesus. They are listed and linked here:

How to See in the Spirit: A Practical Guide on Engaging the Spirit Realm by Michael Van Vlymen and

Seeing in the Spirit Made Simple by Praying Medic.

I feel that when Stephen was being stoned, he saw in the Spirit and looked up into heaven and saw Jesus stand up and welcome him into heaven. (See Acts 7:54–60.) He was overcome with ecstasy. Many of the Christians that suffered in the times of Nero had visions of Jesus just as they were attacked or eaten by a lion. Many members of the early church were practiced in seeing visions, which brought them comfort.

I would encourage believers who are being persecuted to develop the ability to see Jesus and commune with him because the presence of the Holy Spirit and of Jesus will comfort you when you need it.

When I was shipwrecked and floating in the ocean, I didn't meditate on the sharks or the danger. I meditated on Jesus. I knew that I had more missions, more time to keep on going with my ministries. I knew that the shipwreck wasn't the end of my life. You can have perspective by understanding your mission on earth. Without understanding why you are here, you can be in a weak, vulnerable position and can be easily attacked and sidelined.

I had a clear understanding of my mission and why I was on earth. Since I understood my mission so well, I was able to persevere against every sort of attack against me. I really suffered. If you include the verses here of how I suffered in 2 Corinthians 11:23–29, you'll see that I went through so much.

"Are they ministers of Christ?—I speak as a fool—I am more: in labors more abundant, in stripes above measure, in prisons more frequently, in deaths often. From the Jews five times I received forty stripes minus one. Three times I was beaten with rods; once I was stoned; three times I was shipwrecked; a night and a day I have been in the deep; in journeys often, in perils of waters, in perils of robbers, in perils of my own countrymen, in perils of the Gentiles, in perils in the city, in perils in the wilderness, in perils in the sea, in perils among false brethren; in weariness and toil, in sleeplessness often, in hunger and thirst, in fastings often, in cold and nakedness—besides the other things, what comes upon me daily: my deep concern for all the churches. Who is weak, and I am not weak? Who is made to stumble, and I do not burn with indignation?"

I went through so much and endured all these things because I had a clear understanding of my mission, and I had a tremendous relationship with Jesus. Who would think that while floating through the water after a shipwreck, waiting for the tide to take you to land, that you could be walking through heaven and having a vision of heaven? Who would think that you could be conversing with Jesus in heaven?

It's a strange scene, but that's what's possible, and that's how I endured. I recommend that anyone who is experiencing serious persecution endure in this way. There's comfort in the presence of Jesus, in the presence of the Holy Spirit. When you meditate on Jesus, when you see him and meet with him face-to-face, he will bring exceeding joy and comfort in the middle of any troubles that are assailing you.

Question 18 – Why is it important to please God and not men, and how do you learn to be this way?

It takes a little time to develop a relationship with God to such an extent that everything you do pleases God and every action you take is well pleasing to him. You can't just become a Christian and immediately start to please God in everything you do. It takes some time and effort to develop the ability to know what serving the world is and the difference between serving the world and serving God. It takes a while to work out what is well pleasing to God and what the enemy wants you to do.

It takes a little bit of effort to work out how to please God. But once you do work out how to please God, you can walk that way. You can practice this. I would say that many Christians want to please God. I would say that if you ask many Christians if they believe that their life was well pleasing to God, many would say yes.

If you ask them if they're pleasing God as much as they could be, many might say that they don't think that they are. There are levels and different dimensions of pleasing God. Some people are very zealous and passionate about pleasing him. We have had discussions about people who follow the extreme grace movement. Many people in the extreme grace movement are wholly devoted to serving God and pleasing him.

Many zealous, passionate Christians in the legalistic and religious camp will do everything possible to please God. Many people in between both camps who are balanced also know how to please God.

Temptations always exist to please men. Many people stress over what they will say on a Facebook post. They try to consider what people will think of them if they post what is on their mind on

Facebook. They change what they say, depending on how they feel that people will react.

Many people consider what others will think of them when they say something. Rather than posting that people should learn to give God at least 10 percent of their income in an offering, they hold back. There's no excuse for robbing God. People who don't give 10 percent to God lack faith. You could post that. Many people wouldn't post that because it's too direct, and they would be concerned about what their friends might think.

Sometimes you have to do things that make you uncomfortable when you're working closely with the Holy Spirit. Sometimes you have to say things that aren't too comfortable for the hearers to hear. You remember when I said in Galatians 4:16, "Have I therefore become your enemy because I tell you the truth?" I said that because people had issues with what I was teaching.

It's true that people can oppose you when you speak God's truth. You need to decide who you will serve. Will you serve God and his law of love? Will you be loving and correct people when they behave in a way that is not pleasing to God?

People who aren't giving to God are behaving and acting wrongly. Are you going to hold back on what God wants to say? Will you please man and not rock the boat? Correcting a body of believers is a loving thing to do. 2 Timothy 3:16 tells us that the Word of God challenges people and corrects and rebukes people, and it can also be used to encourage people and build them up.

You can be used by God to correct people if you do so in love. When you don't correct others and share words of wisdom and words of correction, you harm them. It's not loving to leave people in their sins, to leave them in disobedience to God and acting contrary to the Word of God and to his purposes.

You need to learn to serve God and say and do what honors him instead of what pleases men. I hope that I answered your questions sufficiently, Nicola.

Question 19 – In Ephesians 2:8–9, you talked about how we are saved by grace and not works but that God created us to do good works. What would you say to Christians about the difference between accepting God's gift of grace and doing works but not doing works to earn salvation?

That's a great question. I have been watching Matthew from heaven, and he understands that this is true too as so much of his life was bound up in religion. Even after he received a measure of freedom, he found himself trying to build up insurance, trying to ensure that he wouldn't go to hell. He used to write many articles and wrote eight hundred and fifty articles published on www.ezinearticles.com simply because he was trying to protect himself and earn his way to heaven.

So many people in the Christian faith do good works in order to reserve their spot in heaven. People commonly do works with that mindset. So many zealous, passionate Christians go out on street corners to save people and lead them to Christ, but they do it with a religious spirit and a religious mindset of needing to save people. They think that in order to inherit the kingdom of God, they need to introduce people to Christ.

You'll find that they will tell you that you have to read your Bible, and you have to go to church, and you have to tithe. You have to do all these things to inherit the kingdom of God. You won't be saved for too long before they'll be dragging you out to witness on the streets and bring other people into that type of legalistic behavior.

Each of us was created by God with a unique destiny and a purpose. Ephesians 2:10 says, "For we are his workmanship, created in Christ Jesus for good works, which God prepared beforehand that we should walk in them."

Every person was created with a purpose and a destiny, created to do wonderful things. You were created to be a fruit-bearing tree. It would be strange for you to be an apple tree and not bear apples. It would be strange for you to be a pear tree and not bear pears. If someone planted you into fertile soil as an apple tree and fertilized you and dug around and watered you, after many years, they would be upset if you weren't producing apples for them.

In the same way, you should bear fruit as a Christian. Your life should bring forth fruit and good works from that fruit. When you learn to love, when you learn to live a life of love and extending love to others, you'll develop good fruit and a lifestyle of good works. It's true that a lifestyle of good works blesses people and leads others closer to the kingdom of God.

Many people are like Matthew was and have this motive for doing good works. They feed the poor; they help homeless people; they make sandwiches and give to the poor. They do all sorts of outreaches for others, but they can do it as part of a works-based salvation for themselves.

They believe that grace plus works equals salvation. They don't realize that they don't need to earn their way to heaven, but their actions should be a natural expression of love coming from them. It's a subtle change, not an overt change that needs to happen in those people. People have to be reintroduced to the love and the grace of Jesus Christ and set free from the bondage of religion and slavery to a set of rules and a certain form of behavior.

A subtle change needs to happen. You can go from spending all your time writing articles and writing books to earn salvation to writing articles and books out of love for God. Works and fruit can flow freely from your life.

Matthew understands this question because he's lived in both camps. It's so much more rewarding to live so that you bear fruit and express the love that you have for God and the love that you have for other people.

This is a great question, Nicola. I hope that I gave you some insight into it.

Question 20 – What went through your heart and mind as you were imprisoned, and what kept you going?

I was imprisoned several times. Once, I was under house arrest, and I had freedom so that I could do Bible studies and meet with people. Another time, toward the end of my life as seen in the movie, *Paul the Apostle*, I was under strict imprisonment, which was worse.

I assume that you're talking about that time and wondering what was going through my heart and mind. I was very pastoral. I planted and started churches and preached to many believers. When I was back in prison, the confinement had me concerned about the believers that I wasn't reaching. So I wrote letters in prison to the churches.

I spent my time contemplating what they were doing and trying to work out the words to help them. I would write them letters. I was constantly in prayer for the churches. I knew many people by name and prayed for them. I prayed for the leaders and the people of the fellowships.

Like I said when I was in the water, when I was shipwrecked, I had visions of heaven so much of the time. I spent a lot of time face-to-face with Jesus. It was true that during my imprisonment, in the hard times, I looked on the face of Jesus. Jesus came down and visited me, and I went to heaven and visited him. I had many times of ecstasy.

You'll find more testimony by John about this if you read the book, *The Apostle John Speaks from Heaven*. You'll find that on Patmos, he spent much time in trances and visions, spending time with Jesus. I also had a supernatural life, the kind of life that every believer should possess and pursue.

If you're reading this book and you have never met Jesus, well, it's your birthright as a believer. Scripture says in Ephesians 2:6 that we're seated in heavenly places. If you're indeed seated in heavenly places, if you're seated next to Christ in heaven, all you need to do is open your spiritual eyes, and you can look around the throne room and meet Jesus and talk to him.

I encourage readers to develop the ability to hear and see Jesus. I encourage them to reach a place where they meet Jesus and interact with him. I did meet with Luke and with other people who came to the prison. I encouraged them and gave them messages for the churches that I loved.

I spent a lot of time praying for the churches and having visions and interacting with Jesus in heaven. The last time I was in prison was when I was close to my death. I spent so much time looking forward to my actual death. I was counting down the days as it were until they were going to put me to death. I am not sure that you would understand this way of thinking unless you had also met Jesus like I had.

I was really excited at the end of my life. If you've suffered before, you'd understand that. Not only the suffering made me look forward to heaven but spending so much time in the courts of heaven with Jesus made me just long for his presence and long to be in heaven.

Question 21 – What do you love most about the Lord Jesus, Father God, and the Holy Spirit?

First of all, I'll talk about the Lord Jesus, my Savior and my Redeemer. I loved his grace. I loved the compassion that he had for me. I could have stayed a wretched man all my life. I could have been an enemy of the church and continued to live my life that way, killing Christians and causing them indescribable grief.

But Jesus had other plans for my life, plans to totally revolutionize me and transform me into a bearer of his light, a bearer of his love. He did a tremendous work in my heart and gave me his heart for people. He truly was the key to my ability to love.

Jesus, through the Holy Spirit, infused his love into me and taught me how to love. What I love most about Jesus is his ability to love and show his love and how he accepts any man, no matter what he's done. Jesus welcomes even the worst sinner into his embrace and warmly hugs him and shows him unconditional love and grace. That's why I love the love of Jesus.

I really love the Father because he treated me like a friend. I was created as a son by the Father, and I fully understood my sonship. The Father treated me like a real friend as any father can be a friend of his child, and the child can flourish under the hand of his father. The friendship that the father displayed to him was really the friendship of God. My friendship with God when I lived on earth meant more than words could ever say to me. We still have that same level of friendship in heaven such that he gives me authority to teach in heaven. He gives me the capacity to love people and free reign to do as I please in heaven.

God is such a reliable friend. I encourage readers to pursue the Father in such a way that he can go beyond being your heavenly Father so that you develop a true and lasting friendship with God.

Jesus is my Savior; Jesus is my love, and his Father is my friend and companion that truly loved and respected me for who I was.

What I love most about the Holy Spirit is that he is the conduit to God. Everything that he is, is of God. Everything that he is, is of the Lord Jesus. All the strong points— his personality, the power, the authority—all of it comes through the Holy Spirit. I love the Holy Spirit for his humility, for his ability to lead and empower and direct my life and comfort me.

The Holy Spirit is like a mother. He is motherly, supportive, loving, nurturing, and a tremendous resource for anyone who wants to live the Christian life. I love the humility of the Holy Spirit. He is equal to God, but he operates at this level that allows you to praise Jesus and the Father, but he doesn't necessarily accept praise from you.

He encourages you to worship Jesus and God, but he doesn't necessarily encourage you to worship him. As I said, he is so humble and an important part of the church going forth today. He's an important part of all the messages that are preached and all the pastors and preachers of every type.

He brings the anointing. He brings the presence of Jesus to meetings. He empowers people. He gives people the ability to move in the nine gifts of the Holy Spirit. He fills people with love. He fills people with the ability to practice the Christian faith.

That's how I feel about the three members of the Trinity.

Matthew's Questions

Question 22 – What do you think about people using your words to prove their point when their point is error? How do you feel about that?

First of all, I want to point you to a scripture that I wrote to Timothy in 2 Timothy 3:16. It says, "All scripture is given by inspiration of God, and is profitable for doctrine, for reproof, for correction, for instruction in righteousness, that the man of God may be complete, thoroughly equipped for every good work."

Scripture is intended to teach people how to live a righteous life and build them up. It's for reproof and correction. When it's used for a different purpose, there's a problem.

I said further on in 2 Timothy 4:2–4, "Preach the word! Be ready in season and out of season. Convince, rebuke, exhort, with all longsuffering and teaching. For the time will come when they will not endure sound doctrine, but according to their own desires, because they have itching ears, they will heap up for themselves teachers; and they will turn their ears away from the truth, and be turned aside to fables."

I shared with Timothy in that passage two thousand years ago that a time would come when people would gather to themselves teachers that taught error. The best way to teach error is to use scripture verses to back up your error. Sadly, the issue is that not many people who walk in error realize that they're in error. People who are deluded don't usually know that they're deluded.

One way to come out of error is to recognize that what you're teaching is not the truth. But how do you do that unless someone brings correction to you? If you're not open to correction, if you don't have leaders, an accountability team, or people around you that can bring correction to you, how can you ever change your ways?

Of course, I'm concerned that major teachers in the world with big ministries have a legalistic teaching and use many of my scriptures to teach legalism and religion, which causes people to be more bound up. Jesus said to the Pharisees in Matthew 23:15 that they go overseas to win a convert and make them even more messed up than they were before they were converted.

The modern-day Pharisee, the modern-day religious Christian, does the same thing. People become excited when they're saved, but when religion and all the rules set in, the person can live this uneventful, condemned life, a life of shame. We all know that there is no condemnation for those in Christ Jesus. (See Romans 8:1.)

On the other end of the scale, some teachers teach a form of grace that's in error, and we've discussed this. They use my scripture verses to teach that error. How do I feel about this? Of course, I feel upset. I warned Timothy that teachers would come who teach error, and the people would have itching ears.

When you have an itching ear, you love to scratch it. Whenever you have something on your body that itches, you feel better when you scratch it. When people listen to teaching that is off and they love the teaching, they love to scratch the itch. The teacher has to continue to bring the same error week after week because the people love it, and they demand it.

I have been upset about these things. It's tough to watch from heaven when so many people fall into two extremes: legalism and hyper-grace. I wish there were more teachers like Shawn Bolz, Andrew Wommack, Kris Valloton, and Rolland Baker that could teach sound theology and sound doctrine and who would correctly use the Bible rather than deciding what they want the people to do and then finding verses to support their opinions. I would rather that they use the Bible to interpret itself and to instruct people instead of approaching a subject the way that they want to and finding verses to back up their views.

I'm very distressed, and yet this was predicted. I knew that this would happen. I predicted it and shared it. Now here we are. People follow teachers today who teach error. These popular teachers have written books and sell out conferences. They have huge churches and huge followings.

I'd encourage you to check out Shawn Bolz, Andrew Wommack, and Rolland Baker. Check out their teachings and see how the truth sits with you.

Question 23 – Do you think that people should learn to speak to the Trinity and have a wonderful relationship with them in addition to reading the Bible?

You have to ask yourselves whether Moses and Abraham knew their Bible really well or if they knew God really well. Abraham lived way before the law was given. The law was given to Moses, one of his descendants, but Abraham lived much earlier than that and had a relationship with God himself. There was no Bible, no written Word for him to follow. He had to depend on his own relationship with God instead.

The same was true of Moses. He had a relationship with God as well. The Israelites at that time had a relationship with God. They didn't have the Bible. Moses is credited with writing the first five books of the Bible. The people of God before Moses didn't have a Bible, and yet they had a relationship with God.

Your Trinity should not be God the Father, Jesus the Son, and the Holy Bible. Instead, your Trinity is God the Father, Jesus the Son, and the Holy Spirit. All Christians need to have a two-way relationship with Jesus Christ so that they can learn how to hear God's voice.

Matthew has a book, *How to Hear God's Voice: Keys to Two-Way Conversational Prayer*, that you can order by clicking the link here. You can learn to hear God's voice. Praying Medic also has a book called, *Hearing God's Voice Made Simple*. Praying Medic has also put together another book with various other writers about God's voice called *God Speaks: Perspectives on Hearing God's Voice*.

You must have a conversational relationship with God and understand God for who he is. You must understand his personality and be able to converse back and forth with him. You must be able to converse with Jesus and even speak to the Holy Spirit. Each member of the Trinity has a different and distinct personality. They also have a different frequency to their voice.

As a Christian, you can learn to discern the voice of Jesus, the voice of the Holy Spirit, and the voice of the Father. You can live an exciting life where you can walk and talk with Jesus. You can learn to walk down the street and have a vision of Jesus so that he is walking and talking to you. As you develop your skills at seeing visions and at walking and talking with Jesus, your faith will grow to an amazing level!

When you go through any type of suffering or tribulation, you really need to be able to walk and talk with Jesus Christ. You also need to develop a relationship with God the Father instead of just talking to God in a one-way conversation, which is how most people pray. You can ask God questions, and he can answer you, and you can talk to each other as friends.

If you want to learn more about two-way conversations with God, you can read Matthew's books on this topic: <u>Conversations with God: Book 1</u>, <u>Conversations with God: Book 2</u>, and <u>Conversations with God: Book 3</u>. You can check them out and read what conversations Matthew had about certain subjects and see how the conversations naturally flow. Matthew has a lot to say and so does God. It's really exciting.

Matthew got to know Jesus first, then God the Father second. He's now developing his ability to talk to and communicate with the Holy Spirit. It's exciting to live a life that's directed by the Holy Spirit, not just through your intuition with a thought to go here or go there or do a certain thing, but for the Holy Spirit to actually speak a sentence to your mind or spirit and direct you to do a certain thing so that you know that the Holy Spirit just told you what to do.

On earth, I had a vibrant relationship with all three members of the Trinity. I saw Jesus all the time in visions. As I've discussed, I went to heaven multiple times. I lived a life that was somewhat like Enoch of the Bible, this totally supernatural life. This is part of your inheritance as a son or a daughter of God.

Everyone seems to be shortchanged when they don't know their rights. If you don't know your rights in society, people can put one over on you and take advantage of you. But when you know your rights as a citizen in society, you have more benefits. The same is true in the spiritual dimension. When you know your rights as a son or daughter, you know that you have the ability to speak to Jesus, God, and the Holy Spirit, have visions, and have heavenly encounters. When you know your birthright, you can take advantage of it and live a more fulfilling and beneficial life.

Question 24 – What are some things that Jesus said to you that encouraged you when you were on earth?

If you've read <u>Great Cloud of Witnesses Speak</u>, you will have heard a similar question asked of the nineteen saints there. In that book, the question was, "What were some things that God said to you that encouraged you?" I answered that question in that book, but this is a slightly different question. "What did Jesus say to you that encouraged you?"

Jesus said that I was an overcomer and that he was proud of me. He explained to me that an overcomer persists and then endures through life against impossible odds.

Quite often, he was speaking to me when I was right in the middle of the hardship. When the men were beating me with rods or when I was being stoned, Jesus was speaking to me and encouraging me that I was an overcomer and that I could endure the extreme torture. What I went through was very, very painful.

One of the saints that Matthew knows from India reported that he saw me in heaven. He reported that my body still bears the scars that happened because of how I was treated on earth. It's true; my body does have the scars that were inflicted on earth.

It was so encouraging when Jesus said that I was an overcomer. It filled my heart with joy when he said that he was proud of me. Many people might assume that I was proud because of how I write and the authority that I write with. The fact remains that I was a humble servant.

I was just so infused with the love of God that I wanted to serve people, build them up, and equip them to go on with their journey.

I had tremendous fruit for my labors. Many people ended up in heaven because of my testimony and because of the work I did.

When Jesus says that he's proud of you and repeats that to you, you are very encouraged. Has Jesus ever said to you, dear reader, that he's proud of you, that he's happy with you, and that he honors you? It's exciting to hear those words from Jesus. I was especially impressed that he called me an overcomer because in a way, he was prophesying through his words and calling forth my identity. He was saying, "I believe in you. I'm proud of you, and you will overcome everything that comes against you."

That's why I could say in Philippians 4:13, "you can do all things through Christ who gives you strength." I was able to write that because I lived it out. I could do everything through Christ who gave me strength.

It's a tremendous honor to be given the opportunity to serve Christ. I said that I was a bond slave to Christ. I had commissioned myself to be a slave to Jesus Christ. It brought me great honor.

His encouragement that I was an overcomer really carried me, carried me on eagle's wings. He gave me a supernatural, life-affirming word. He told me many other things, and I had many conversations with him. I walked and talked with him and had a mystical relationship with him. He said many amazing things to me.

I encourage you to learn how to hear from Jesus, talk to Jesus, and start your own conversation with Jesus. Let him share what he thinks about you with you. If you read Matthew's books, *Conversations With God: Book 1*, *Conversations with God: Book 2, and Conversations with God: Book 3*, you'll see that God is constantly telling Matthew that he's proud of him, and he's happy with him, and he loves him. On a couple of occasions, God actually cries because of his love for Matthew.

When you have those encounters with Jesus and with God, you remember those things. You remember the precious things that happen. You remember seeing God face-to-face and seeing him cry. Matthew remembers that and treasures it in his heart.

I remember bringing Jesus to tears. I remember Jesus's sweet voice when I was being stoned and being beaten with rods. His life-assuring words, saying that he's proud of me, sustained me and took me to another place even in the midst of my pain. I almost escaped the pain because I was in ecstasy in my spiritual encounter with Jesus. Jesus said some lovely things to me.

Question 25 – You have shared that you lived a supernatural life on earth. Do you feel everyone should live this sort of life?

Well, the mere recording of this book is a supernatural event. Being close to Jesus is supernatural. The ability to hear Jesus and interviewing saints at his request is supernatural. Matthew lives a very supernatural life.

The very fact that you, the reader, are reading this book means that you're interested in the supernatural. You're interested in more of God. So many people in the Christian world settle in life. They sit in pews and go back to church week after week and settle for a dull, boring life. But some people are hungry, and they pursue everything that God has for them. They pursue God himself. These are the kinds of people that I feel should go after the supernatural things of God.

You, as a reader, want to learn how to hear from God, from Jesus, and from the Holy Spirit. You, as a reader, want to learn to prophesy and share messages with people that come from Jesus and the Holy Spirit. You, as a people, want to learn how to go to heaven, have visions of Jesus, and engage with the supernatural. These will all add a whole new dimension to your life.

I'm not sure how I could have endured being stoned and beaten with rods if I didn't have a supernatural relationship with Jesus. Of course, many people have gone through those things without a supernatural relationship with him. Many people have been persecuted without talking to Jesus. I don't own the rights to severe persecution. I'm not the only person who was beaten, stoned, and seriously hurt, but I can say that my supernatural life, my ability to hear from Jesus, and experience trances and visions, really helped me out and added another dimension to my walk of faith.

I encourage you to pursue these things. If they are natural for Matthew, if he can see me standing here beside him, speaking through him, if he can see Jesus in the room and see angels and saints of the Bible standing by, why can't you? He doesn't have a university or a Bible college education. He doesn't have the best education. He even failed English in high school.

If he can experience Jesus and the supernatural as just a simple person without any education, why can't you? What's holding you back? I know that Jesus wants you to hear from him. I know that Jesus wants you to see him. I know that as you read this book, there's a presence in your room. As I say this and you're reading, you can even sense my presence in your room.

Why don't you say hello and see if I'll talk back to you? I will visit everyone who has the faith to say hello. I want to see you living a supernatural life and invite you to experience it.

I encourage you to read the books suggested in these pages. I encourage you to spend your money and your time pursuing the supernatural because it will add another dimension to your life. It will add flavor and character. It will fill out your spiritual muscles like a gym helps to fill out natural muscles, and you can exercise your faith and become more robust and build your character.

It is really a wonderful expression of faith to be able to see, walk, and communicate with angels, saints, Jesus, and the Father. It adds another dimension to the Bible to not only read of angelic encounters in the Bible but to have your own memories to go back to, your own experiences with the angelic.

You can not only read that Jesus met Moses and Elijah on the Mount of Transfiguration, but you can have your own encounters with saints on earth. The more that you develop in the supernatural and the more experience that you have with the supernatural, the more the Bible will come alive to you.

Question 26 – What do you say to people that find your teachings hard to understand? What should they do?

2 Peter 3:15–16 says, "And consider that the longsuffering of our Lord is salvation—as also our beloved brother Paul, according to the wisdom given to him, has written to you, as also in all his epistles, speaking in them of these things, in which are some things hard to understand, which untaught and unstable people twist to their own destruction, as they do also the rest of the Scriptures."

Peter shared with his readers that I've written some things that are hard to understand. He also confirms here that certain teachers twist what I shared to distort and mislead people. We previously discussed that certain teachers twist my scriptures and teach people incorrectly.

Peter said that some of my writings were hard to understand. Matthew was reading through the Bible one time, the New Testament. He'd read all of my letters, including Hebrews. When he reached 2 Peter 3:15–16 and read what Peter wrote, Matthew agreed with him. He said, "Yes, Paul was hard to understand. I don't understand much of Paul." Jesus said to him at that point, "Go back and read the Gospels, and stay in the Gospels until I say so." Matthew went back and read the Gospels for four years.

I suggest that you start to read the Gospels too. Start to ask questions of Jesus such as, "In this situation, how did you feel? Why did you say what you said? What did you mean when you said this?" Ask Jesus questions. Learn to speak to him.

You'll find that if you spend the time with Jesus one on one speaking with him, you'll have a solid comprehension of the Christian faith. Of course, you can read the <u>fifty commands of Jesus</u> listed here. You can read Matthew's book, <u>*The Parables of Jesus Made Simple: Updated and Expanded Edition*</u>, here, which will teach you what Jesus was saying in his parables and give you an overall understanding of Jesus's life message.

The four Gospels provide plenty of content for you to read. But you can read Peter, John, and other parts of the Bible as well. When you have a complete understanding of the Gospels and a solid understanding of what Jesus taught, you'll find my epistles easier to understand. I'll repeat this. When you have an understanding of what Jesus taught, you'll have a better understanding of what I taught.

That's how it worked out for Matthew. That's how he walks and talks like Jesus because he learned so much about Jesus. That's one of the reasons he hasn't quoted a lot of scriptures from me in this book. He does not want to quote a lot of scriptures to prove points as he has been hurt and burnt by wrong teaching. He doesn't read the Bible as often as people think that he should have.

There's a lot to the Bible: Proverbs, Psalms, and Isaiah, for example. Isaiah's a great book to read. You can read many books apart from my letters and my epistles. That's what I encourage you to do.

Find a great Bible commentary. Read what I've written with the help of a commentary. They can share their opinion of what I was saying. A human instructor will help you to understand some of my teachings.

Matthew found that studying Jesus's teachings for many years really helped him. In some places, like in Romans, he still struggles with some of what I have to say. He's not ashamed that I've said that because it's true.

You shouldn't be ashamed personally to admit that some of what I've said is hard to understand because even Peter, the mighty apostle that he was, found that what I had to say was quite difficult for him to understand. He felt so strongly about it that he even wrote to his followers and said, "Paul has written some things that are hard to understand." I hope that you are impressed with that answer, Matthew.

Question 27 – Have you seen the future of earth from heaven? What does it look like?

That's a very interesting question, Matthew. A camp of believers in the world believes the dominion theory, which means that Christians will rise up in to all areas of influence and take control of the earth. They believe in sheep nations and goat nations. They believe the Christians will lead the sheep nations.

Another camp of people believes in darkness coming to the world, the rise of antichrist, the mark of the beast, and the tribulation. They have a very poor and unhopeful outlook on the world. The people who believe in the dominion theory utterly reject the ideas of the people that believe in the book of Revelation or how Revelation will play out. The people who believe in Revelation, the antichrist, and the tribulation have issues with the people who believe that everything will be fine and dandy and that the world is going to get better and better.

The truth is in the middle. The world will become harder and harder for Christians to live in. Persecution will come. Life will become darker.

This is true, but a rising number of Christians will shine, have light, and have influence in the world. The truth is somewhat in the middle of both understandings. If you understand both camps, the truth is found in the middle.

Like with anything, there has to be balance. It will be an exciting time for people who are walking with Jesus, obeying him, and living their life dedicated to him with their passion and their hunger for all things Jesus. As the world becomes darker and more depressing, the Christians who carry the light of Christ will shine brighter. In the future, it will be easier to win people to the Christian faith. When life becomes dark and desperate and circumstances become harder to live in and when trouble seems to break out in the world, the influence of Christians will count for a lot.

The Christian church, the believers who aren't part of a church that's dead or lukewarm, these Christians are living vibrant, glorified, happy, Spirit-filled, presence-filled lives. They will attract people to themselves like moths are attracted to a flame. You will be able to counsel people who are going through difficult times and lead them to the hope that's in Christ. A time will come when ordinary Christians will learn how to heal and how to prophesy. They will influence people at their work and those they do life with. So many Christians will rise up and become part of an army that will invade the earth and convince the earth of Jesus's life and the fact that Jesus is living and alive.

A revival will hit the world, including stadium ministries. Many people will be saved. There will be a resurgence of Christianity. This resurgence, this light, and this breaking out of the Christian faith scare Satan so much. It will cause Satan to bring on the evil in the world, the destruction, and the darkness because he is so scared of the light. He wants to suppress the light that is coming.

That's good news for the world and for people who are sixty, fifty, and younger because you will live a life that counts for something. You will live a life that breaks out and is responsible for saving other people's lives and bringing more people into the kingdom of God.

You're fast approaching a time where religion and stale Christianity just won't work. Many churches will have their lampstands taken by the Holy Spirit. They will just flicker out. Many religious churches that are built on tradition will just fade away.

Only the zealous, passionate Christian churches will flourish. Only the passionate Christians will go places and do things. If you are reading this book, you're probably in that group of people that will flourish and do mighty exploits in the world as it says in Daniel 11:32.

Question 28 – How does a person make a mark on society like you did?

It's vitally important in this world for you to realize why you're here and to understand your purpose. Certain people are born to be evangelists. Others are born to be teachers, prophets, and pastors.

Still others are destined to be florists, basketball players, professors, and teachers in high schools. All sorts of professions are in the world. It's your job to work out why you're here—not just your job, but what your purpose is on earth.

You can learn to prophesy, hang around with prophets, and receive glimpses of your destiny through each prophecy. You can read Matthew's book, *Finding Your Purpose in Christ*. Read other books on that subject to learn your purpose in Christ because you're born for a reason. You are born to make a mark on society.

You were born for a reason. God created you for a unique purpose. It would be a shame for you to go through your whole life without realizing and understanding your purpose. If you don't know your purpose, you can't walk in it. If you don't know why you're here, you can never complete your destiny on earth.

You can look at some people like Michael Jackson, who's in heaven now. He lived out his purpose and was born to be a musician. He changed a lot of people's lives. Steve Jobs also made it to heaven because of people's prayers. He lived on earth and created Apple and Pixar Animation. He lived out his purpose and made a dent in the world, made a difference to the world. Matthew's using an Apple computer to record this book. Apple is a powerful product and was the creation of Steve Jobs.

Mark Zuckerberg created Facebook. The way people interact with each other has totally changed because of Facebook. Christian churches have totally changed how people market events. Mark Zuckerberg is living out his purpose, and the list can go on.

The owner of the best Italian restaurant in your city is living his purpose. A waitress in that restaurant might be studying acting and waiting tables to earn a living, pay for her acting classes, and working to pass them. People have all sorts of purposes on earth.

You have to seek God until you find the purpose that he has for you. You can contact a life coach, such as Doug Addison or Jeremy Lopez. You can pay for a session of life coaching and ask them what your purpose is or discuss your likes and dislikes with them and come to a decision of what your purpose is. It's worth spending the money to find that out.

Matthew recently started counseling. His counselor did a destiny scroll with him that told what his destiny was with nine different points of what he's called to do. It talks about what Matthew's currently doing plus what he will be doing in the future. It's really encouraging to him, and it gives him a reason to persist and go through what might be difficult counseling to endure and to persevere because he has such a bright future. See [this link](#) for more information.

It's important for you to know your purpose. When you know your purpose, then you can make a mark on society.

If this is the first book you've read by Matthew, you can look on Amazon and check out all the books that interest you that Matthew's written. He talks a lot about purpose, destiny, and the things of God in his books. A person needs to transform their life and let go of the world and its lusts, let go of the things of the world and the patterns of the world. Pursue Christ. Pursue his will, his purpose, and his destiny for your life.

I know that this book has a lot of information to take in and to understand. Like anything in life, it takes practice and determination to have a breakthrough. I encourage you to read this book more than once and find the gems in it for yourself.

Question 29 – What are your final words?

I would like to encourage you all to get to know Jesus by reading Matthew's books, including:

- *The Parables of Jesus Made Simple: Updated and Expanded Edition*,
- *Jesus Speaking Today*,
- *Finding Intimacy with Jesus Made Simple*,
- *Conversations with God: Book 1*,
- *Conversations with God: Book 2*, and
- *Conversations with God: Book 3*.

Learn how to have back-and-forth conversations with Jesus in the following books: *How to Hear God's Voice: Keys to Two-Way Conversational Prayer* **by Matthew Robert Payne,** *Hearing God's Voice Made Simple* **by Praying Medic, and** *God Speaks: Perspectives on Hearing God's Voice* by Praying Medic.

I want to encourage you to learn how to see in the spirit and how to have visions by reading Michael Van Vlymen's book and Praying Medic's book on that subject. I encourage you to pursue your destiny and learn what your purpose is by reading *Finding Your Purpose in Christ*. I encourage you to learn to walk under an open heaven. You can read about that in Matthew's book, *Walking under an Open Heaven*.

It has been an honor to speak to you, and it's been a real privilege to come down and answer questions from Mary, Nicola, and Matthew. I know that it's a real joy for both Mary and Nicola to have their questions answered. I pray that this book has been encouraging for you, dear reader, and that you've learned some things from it.

I'm just a simple guy. It's a privilege to come to earth and speak to people that I love. If you're reading this book, I want to say this to you right now. Know that I'm in your realm right now, and I'm watching you. You might stop reading and say hello and listen to my voice in your spirit.

Some of you might be able to start a conversation with me right here and now. Understand that I know everyone who will read this book, and I will personally be in your room when you're reading it. As you're reading this sentence, I'll be visiting you. Know that I love you and that I'm praying for you. I encourage you to pursue Jesus with everything that you have.

I want you to know that Jesus is the way, the truth, and the life, and there is no way to heaven except through him. (See John 14:6.) I want you to know that Jesus is my bedrock. I love him, and he's my source. I want you to know that he will guide you and direct you with the help of the Holy Spirit, who is there to counsel you, teach you, and lead you.

I envision that as you close this book, you might have more questions for me. I encourage you to develop a relationship with Jesus. You can access me and start to speak to me and ask me a question yourself. With that said, have a great day.

I'd love to hear from you

One of the ways that you can bless me as a writer is by writing an honest and candid review of my book on Amazon. I always read the reviews of my books, and I would love to hear what you have to say about this one.

Before I buy a book, I read the reviews first. You can make an informed decision about a book when you have read enough honest reviews from readers. One way to help me sell this book and to give me positive feedback is by writing a review for me. It doesn't cost you a thing but helps me and the future readers of this book enormously.

To read my blog, request a life-coaching session, request your own personal prophecy, to receive a personal message from your angel, or to receive your destiny scroll, you can also visit my website at http://personal-prophecy-today.com All of the funds raised through my ministry website will go toward the books that I write and self-publish.

To write to me about this book or to share any other thoughts, please feel free to contact me at my personal email address at survivors.sanctuary@gmail.com

You can also friend request me on Facebook at Matthew Robert Payne. Please send me a message if we have no friends in common as a lot of scammers now send me friend requests.

You can also do me a huge favor and share this book on Facebook as a recommended book to read. This will help me and other readers.

How to Sponsor a Book Project

If you have been blessed by this book, you might consider sponsoring a book for me. It normally costs me between fifteen hundred and two thousand dollars or more to produce each book that I write, depending on the length of the book.

If you seek the Holy Spirit about financing a book for me, I know that the Lord would be eternally grateful to you. Consider how much this book has blessed you and then think of hundreds or even thousands of people who would be blessed by a book of mine. As you are probably aware, the vast majority of my books are ninety-nine cents on Kindle, which proves to you that book writing is indeed a ministry for me and not a money-making venture. I would be very happy if you supported me in this.

If you have any questions for me or if you want to know what projects I am currently working on that your money might finance, you can write to me at survivors.sanctuary@gmail.com and ask me for more information. I would be pleased to give you more details about my projects.

You can sow any amount to my ministry by simply sending me money via the PayPal link at this address: http://personal-prophecy-today.com/support-my-ministry

You can be sure that your support, no matter the amount, will be used for the publishing of helpful Christian books for people to read.

Other Books by Matthew Robert Payne

The Prophetic Supernatural Experience

Prophetic Evangelism Made Simple

Your Identity in Christ

His Redeeming Love: A Memoir

Writing and Self-Publishing Christian Nonfiction

Coping with your Pain and Suffering

Living for Eternity

Jesus Speaking Today

Great Cloud of Witnesses Speak

My Radical Encounters with Angels

Finding Intimacy with Jesus Made Simple

My Radical Encounters with Angels: Book Two

A Beginner's Guide to the Prophetic

Michael Jackson Speaks from Heaven

7 Keys to Intimacy with Jesus

Conversations with God: Book 1

Optimistic Visions of Revelation

Conversations with God: Book 2

Finding Your Purpose in Christ

Influencing your World for Christ: Practical Everyday Evangelism

Deep Calls unto Deep: Answering Questions on the Prophetic

My Visits to the Galactic Council of Heaven

The Parables of Jesus Made Simple: Updated and Expanded Edition

Great Cloud of Witnesses Speak: Old and New

Walking under an Open Heaven

A Message from My Angel: Book 1

Conversations with God: Book 3

Interviews with the Two Witnesses: Enoch and Elijah Speak

Gaining Freedom from Sex Addictions: Breaking Free of Pornography and Prostitutes

Mary Magdalene Speaks from Heaven: A Divine Revelation

Princess Diana Speaks from Heaven: A Divine Revelation

How to Hear God's Voice: Keys to Conversational Two-Way Prayer

Apostle John Speaks from Heaven: A Divine Revelation

What I Believe

Great Cloud of Witnesses Speak: God's Generals

Apostle Peter Speaks from Heaven: A Divine Revelation

King David Speaks from Heaven: A Divine Revelation

Twenty-Two Signs that You're Called to Be a Prophet

Nineteen Scriptures to Change Your Life Forever

Five Keys to Successful Writing: How I Write One Book per Month

My Visits to Heaven: Lessons Learned

You can find my published books on my Amazon author page here: http://tinyurl.com/jq3h893

Upcoming Books:

Mary Magdalene Speaks from Heaven Book 2: A Divine Revelation

About Matthew Robert Payne

Matthew was raised in a Baptist church and was led to the Lord at the tender age of eight. He has experienced some pain and darkness in his life, which have given him a deep compassion and love for all people.

Today, he's a founding member and admin of a Facebook group called "Prophetic Training Group," and he invites you to join him there. Matthew has a commission from the Lord to train up prophets and to mentor others in the Christian faith. He does this through his Facebook posts and by writing relevant books on the Christian faith.

God originally commissioned him to write at least fifty books in his life, but that has now increased to ninety books. He spends his days writing and earning the money to self-publish. You can support him by donating money at http://personal-prophecy-today.com or by requesting any of the other services available through his ministry website.

Recently, the Lord has put it on his heart to start his own publishing company for other people's books to be called Christian Book Publishing USA. It is Matthew's hope to help some people self-publish their books in the future.

It is Matthew's prayer that this book has blessed you, and he hopes it will lead you into a deeper and more intimate relationship with God.

www.ingramcontent.com/pod-product-compliance
Lightning Source LLC
LaVergne TN
LVHW051153080426
835508LV00021B/2601